Peter Pan

About Wise & Wide

- A systematic 6-level English reading program based on Lexile® measures
- Diverse and interesting topics chosen from the elementary curriculums of Korea and English speaking western countries
- Well-written books in various forms including fiction stories, descriptive texts, and classics retold
- The informative but original fiction stories grab your interest, leading to the easy and clear understanding of the educational content.
- Improve thinking skills with solid after-reading activities at all levels of the series.

Wise & Wide is a 6-level English reading program that consists of 60 books and each level is systematically divided by Lexile® measures. The Lexile® Framework for Reading is the most popular reading measuring system in American formal education curriculums and many English programs. Over 20 out of 50 states in the U.S. mark Lexile® measures directly on students' final report cards and over 300 well-known publishers adopt and use Lexile® measures.

Experience many kinds of readings written by professional writers from the U.S. and England. They used interesting topics that were carefully chosen after analyzing elementary curriculums from around the world including Korea, the U.S., England, and Australia among many others. Comprehensive after-reading activities including graphic organizers, speaking tasks, and After-reading Tests are ready for you.

Levels in the series and their corresponding Lexile® measures

Level	Lexile® measures	U.S. Grade
Level 1	Below 200L	Pre K - K
Level 2	190L - 400L	Lower Grade 1
Level 3	350L - 530L	Upper Grade 1
Level 4	420L - 650L	Grade 2
Level 5	520L - 940L	Grade 3 - 4
Level 6	830L - 1070L	Grade 5 - 6

* Smart Readers: Wise & Wide level 1 is applicable to the preschool level in the U.S.

* The source of the relationship between Lexile® measures and U.S. school grades: CCSS(Common Core State Standards) FOR ENGLISH LANGUAGE ARTS, APPENDIX A (2012, which is used by 45 states in the U.S.)

Topic List

	Level 1	Level 2	Level 3	Level 4	Level 5	Level 6
Book 1	Science>Biology: The hibernation of animals Story	Science>Biology: Living and nonliving things Story	Science>Biology> Animals & the Environment: Sea otters Story	Environment> Living with nature: The diver & the persimmon tree Story	Science>Biology> Animal: Amazing animals of the Amazon Story	Science>Biology: Germs, transmitted diseases Story
Book 2	Literature> World classics: Aesop's fables Story	Literature> Traditional fairy tale: Old tales about stones Story	Social Studies> Economy: To run a business to make and save money Story	Science>Biology> Plants: Photosynthesis Story	Science>Earth science: Earth's layers, earthquakes, volcanoes, and earth's atmosphere Report	Mathematics> Sequence: The golden ratio & the Fibonacci sequence Story
Book 3	Science>Physics: How shadows are formed Story	Literature> World classics: Peter Pan Story	Science>Scientific technology: Nanobots Story	Literature>Myths: World's creation stories Story	Literature> Legend: The story of King Arthur Story	Literature>Myths: Constellation myths Story
Book 4	Literature> Traditional literature: The Talmud Story	Science>Biology> Animal: Polar bears Story	Science>Biology> Animal: Mountain gorillas Story	Social Studies> Cultural anthropology: Amazing ancient cultures of the world Story	Science> Earth science: Clouds and weather Story	Literature> Human & animals: The friendship between a girl and a horse Story
Book 5	Social Studies> Ethics: Rules in daily life Story	Science>Biology: The five senses Report	Social Studies> Cultural anthropology: Astonishing festivals Report	Art>Music: Stories from two operas Story	Social Studies> World culture & history: The Renaissance Story	Sports> Board sports: Surfing & snowboarding Story
Book 6	Social Studies> World geography & travel: Tourist attractions around the world Story	Science>Biology> Animal: Dinosaurs Story	Science> Astronomy: The solar system Story	Social Studies> People: Three great people who overcame hardships Story	Science>Scientific technology: The wonderful world of robots Report	Art>Music: Composers of the Romantic Era Report
Book 7	Science> Space science: The life of astronauts Report	Social Studies> Cultural anthropology: Mythological monsters from around the world Report	Mathematics> Elementary mathematics: Numbers, measurement, shapes and data Report	Science & Social Studies> Technology & culture: Inventions from around the world Report	Art>Works of art: Famous paintings Report	Social Studies> Human & animals: Animals in action for human Report
Book 8	Social Studies> Cultural anthropology: Various living cultures of the world Story	Art>Music: Instruments in the orchestra Story	Social Studies> Life safety: Learning and using outdoor survival skills Story	Social Studies> History: The California Gold Rush Report	Social Studies & Science> Psychology: Psychology in everyday life Story	Literature> World classics: The Merchant of Venice Story
Book 9	Social Studies> Jobs: Interviews about jobs Report	Science>Scientific technology: Developments in technology in different times Story	Social Studies> Politics>Election: Running for 3rd grade class president Story	Literature> World classics: Stories of Sherlock Holmes Story	Literature> World classics: Adrift in the Pacific Story	Social Studies> History & People: Great world leaders in history Report
Book 10	Literature>Traditional fairy tale: Eastern and Western folk tales on the same theme Story	Sports>Winter sports: Various aspects of some Winter Olympic sports Report	Literature> World classics: Short stories by O. Henry Story	Sports> Ball games: Various aspects of popular ball games Report	Social Studies> History: Famous events that changed world history Report	Art & Social Studies> Art: Stories about the creation, distribution, and preservation of paintings Report

How to Use This Book

•Before Reading

You can easily find the topic and what kind of story you are about to read.

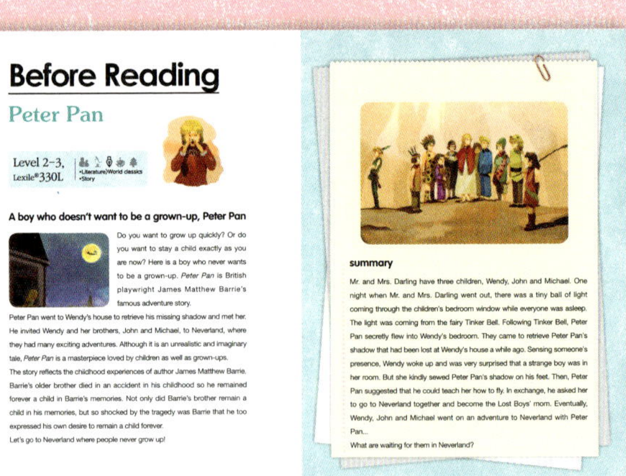

•The text

All the stories were written by professional writers from the U.S. and England, so you will read authentic and appropriate English sentences and expressions in every book in the series.

•Pop Quiz

Check out right away if you understand what you have just read by solving a pop quiz that checks your comprehension.

•Key Words

The key words and expressions on each page are listed for you to easily study them.

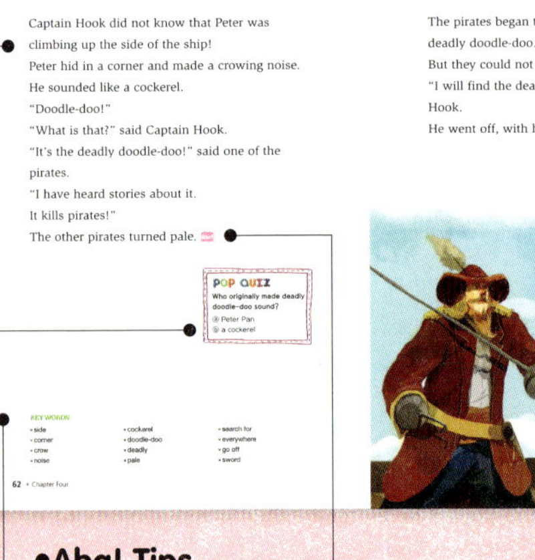

•Aha! Tips

Download free Korean explanations at *www.ihappyhouse.co.kr* for all of the sentences marked with "Aha!". These explain cultural, scientific, and economic knowledge or they deal with aspects of English such as grammatical structures or idiomatic expressions. There are lots of "Aha! Tips" to help you understand the text.

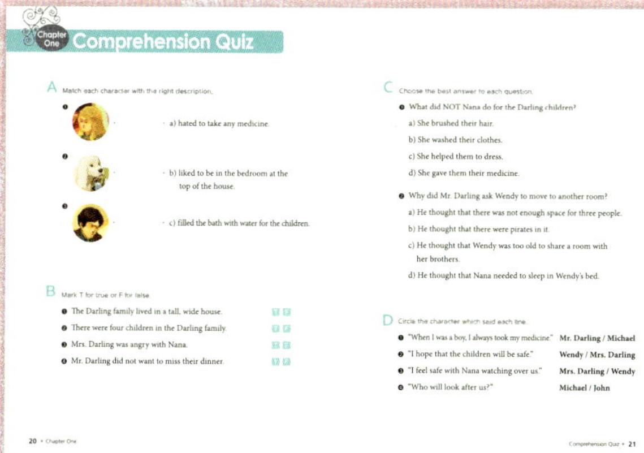

•Comprehension Quiz

After reading one chapter, solve various questions to find out if you fully understand the content.

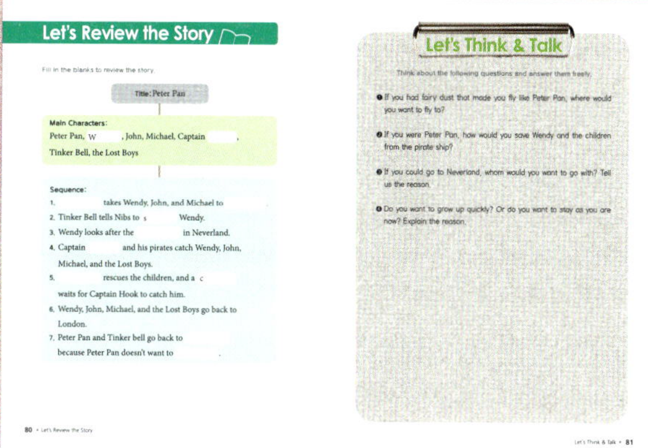

•Let's Review the Story /
•Let's Think & Talk

Fill in the blanks in the organizer to summarize the whole story. Express your own thinking and feelings about the story by answering the questions. You can build up logic and reasoning skills for your essay examinations in the future.

Appendix

Audio CD
In the CD audio book form, the texts are read vividly by American professional voice actors.

After-reading Test
Solve an additionally provided After-reading Test for each book.

The Korean translation, Answer Keys, a Word Quiz, a Word List, and Aha! Tips for each book
You can download them for free at *www.ihappyhouse.co.kr*

Before Reading

Peter Pan

A boy who doesn't want to be a grown-up, Peter Pan

Do you want to grow up quickly? Or do you want to stay a child exactly as you are now? Here is a boy who never wants to be a grown-up. *Peter Pan* is British playwright James Matthew Barrie's famous adventure story.

Peter Pan went to Wendy's house to retrieve his missing shadow and met her. He invited Wendy and her brothers, John and Michael, to Neverland, where they had many exciting adventures. Although it is an unrealistic and imaginary tale, *Peter Pan* is a masterpiece loved by children as well as grown-ups.

The story reflects the childhood experiences of author James Matthew Barrie. Barrie's older brother died in an accident in his childhood so he remained forever a child in Barrie's memories. Not only did Barrie's brother remain a child in his memories, but so shocked by the tragedy was Barrie that he too expressed his own desire to remain a child forever.

Let's go to Neverland where people never grow up!

Summary

Mr. and Mrs. Darling have three children, Wendy, John and Michael. One night when Mr. and Mrs. Darling went out, there was a tiny ball of light coming through the children's bedroom window while everyone was asleep. The light was coming from the fairy Tinker Bell. Following Tinker Bell, Peter Pan secretly flew into Wendy's bedroom. They came to retrieve Peter Pan's shadow that had been lost at Wendy's house a while ago. Sensing someone's presence, Wendy woke up and was very surprised that a strange boy was in her room. But she kindly sewed Peter Pan's shadow on his feet. Then, Peter Pan suggested that he could teach her how to fly. In exchange, he asked her to go to Neverland together and become the Lost Boys' mom. Eventually, Wendy, John and Michael went on an adventure to Neverland with Peter Pan...

What are waiting for them in Neverland?

Contents

Peter Pan

Peter Pan

Time to Grow Up

The Darling family lived in the city of London. 

They lived in a tall, narrow house.

There were three children in the family.

Wendy was the oldest.

She had two brothers, called John and Michael.

The children slept in a bedroom at the top of the house.

Wendy told them stories about strange lands.

Their bedroom was a happy place.

Mr. and Mrs. Darling loved their children.

But they needed help to look after them.

"I do not have much money.

I cannot pay someone to look after you," Mr.

Darling told them.

So he bought a big, friendly dog called Nana.

She looked after the children well.

Nana brushed their hair.

She helped them to dress.

She gave them their medicine.

She even filled the bath with water for them.

KEY WORDS

- **can** (= be able to)
- **pay** (pay-paid-paid)
- **so**
- **buy** (buy-bought-bought)
- **friendly**
- **well**
- **brush one's hair**
- **dress**
- **medicine**
- **even**
- **fill**
- **bath**
- **get ready to go out** (get-got-gotten)
- **too ... to ~**
- **share**
- **shall**
- **of one's own**
- **have fun**
- **safe**
- **watch over**

One evening, Mr. and Mrs. Darling were getting ready to go out.

They went into the children's bedroom.

"Wendy, you are too old to share a room with your brothers," said Mr. Darling.

"Tomorrow, you shall have a room of your own."

"But I like it in here!" said Wendy.

"We have fun together.

I feel safe with Nana watching over us."

Wendy did not want to grow up.

When she was about to tell her father, he shouted, "Look at my trousers!"

His smart trousers were covered with long, white dog hairs.

"Why do we have a dog to take care of our children?" he shouted.

"Because she looks after them so well," said Mrs. Darling.

Just then, Nana appeared.

She had some medicine for Michael.

"Time to take your medicine," she said. `Aha!`

KEY WORDS

- be about to + *Verb*
- shout
- look at
- trousers
- smart
- be covered with

- take care of (take-took-taken)
- because
- just then
- appear
- take a medicine

Michael frowned.

"I don't want to take it." he said.

"When I was a boy, I always took my medicine,"
said Mr. Darling.

"You must do the same."

This was not true.

Mr. Darling hated to take any medicine.

Wendy knew where Mr. Darling kept his
medicine.

She went to fetch it.

"You can show Michael how to be brave," she
said.

Mr. Darling did not want to take the medicine.

He poured it into Nana's bowl.

Nana began to drink it!

- frown
- always
- must (= have to)
- same
- true
- hate
- know (know-knew-known)
- keep (keep-kept-kept)
- fetch

- show (show-showed-shown)
- how to + *Verb*
- brave
- pour
- bowl
- begin (begin-began-begun)
- think (think-thought-thought)
- funny
- joke

- mean (mean-meant-meant)
- ashamed
- outside
- still
- guard
- take
- downstairs
- tie
- doghouse

Mr. Darling thought it was a funny joke.

"That was a mean thing to do!" said Wendy.

Mr. Darling felt ashamed.

"Nana must go and sleep outside!" he said.

"But who will look after us?" cried Michael.

"Nana can still guard the house," said Mr. Darling.

He took Nana downstairs.

He tied her to the doghouse.

After a while, Mrs. Darling came out.

She looked up at the window.

"I hope that the children will be safe," she said.

Nana barked.

It was a bark that meant danger was near.

"Don't you think we should stay at home?" asked
Mrs. Darling.

"No, I do not," said Mr. Darling.

"Now let us go, or we will miss our dinner."

In the bedroom, Wendy lay in bed.

The curtains were open, and she could see the stars.

Everything was quiet.

John and Michael were asleep.

The window was open a little.

Wendy heard Nana barking.

She wondered why Nana was barking.

But, she fell asleep soon.

POP QUIZ

How did Nana express that danger was near?

ⓐ She took her medicine.
ⓑ She barked.

KEY WORDS

- after a while
- come out (come-came-come)
- look up
- hope
- bark
- danger

- near
- should
- stay at home
- let us (let-let-let)
- or
- miss

- lie (lie-lay-lain)
- quiet
- asleep
- hear
- wonder
- soon

Comprehension Quiz

A Match each character with the right description.

❶ 

❷ 

❸ 

- a) hated to take any medicine.

- b) liked to be in the bedroom at the top of the house.

- c) filled the bath with water for the children.

B Mark T for true or F for false.

❶ The Darling family lived in a tall, wide house. T F

❷ There were four children in the Darling family. T F

❸ Mrs. Darling was angry with Nana. T F

❹ Mr. Darling did not want to miss their dinner. T F

C Choose the best answer to each question.

❶ What did NOT Nana do for the Darling children?

a) She brushed their hair.

b) She washed their clothes.

c) She helped them to dress.

d) She gave them their medicine.

❷ Why did Mr. Darling ask Wendy to move to another room?

a) He thought that there was not enough space for three people.

b) He thought that there were pirates in it.

c) He thought that Wendy was too old to share a room with her brothers.

d) He thought that Nana needed to sleep in Wendy's bed.

D Circle the character which said each line.

❶ "When I was a boy, I always took my medicine." **Mr. Darling / Michael**

❷ "I hope that the children will be safe." **Wendy / Mrs. Darling**

❸ "I feel safe with Nana watching over us." **Mrs. Darling / Wendy**

❹ "Who will look after us?" **Michael / John**

A Strange Visitor

Suddenly, a tiny ball of light flew in through the window.

A strange boy flew in after it.

He was dressed in feathers and leaves.

His name was Peter Pan.

"Tinker Bell!" he whispered.

The light flew over and landed on his hand.

It was a fairy.

"What is it?" she asked.

"Where is my shadow?"

Peter looked around the room.

Tinker Bell's voice sounded like tiny bells.

"It is in there," she said.

She pointed at a chest of drawers.

Peter threw Tinker Bell into the air.

He ran to the drawers and began to look inside them.

Tinker Bell went to see what he was doing.

Peter shut her in a drawer by mistake!

KEY WORDS

- visitor
- suddenly
- tiny
- a ball of light
- fly in (fly-flew-flown)
- through
- be dressed in
- feather
- leaf
- whisper
- fly over
- fairy
- shadow
- look around
- sound
- point
- a chest of drawers
- throw (throw-threw-thrown)
- inside
- shut (shut-shut-shut)
- by mistake

At last, Peter found his shadow.

It was folded like a piece of thin, black material.

Unknown to Wendy, Peter had visited her house before.

He had come through the window one night.

Nana had chased him and caught his shadow.

She had folded it up and put it in the drawer.

- at last
- find (find-found-found)
- fold
- a piece of
- material
- unknown to

- visit
- come through
- chase
- catch (catch-caught-caught)
- stick (stick-stuck-stuck)
- onto

- try to + *Verb*
- soap
- work
- wake up (wake-woke-woken)
- surprised

Peter was so happy when he found his shadow.

But he did not know how to stick it back onto his feet.

He tried to stick his shadow on with some soap.

But it did not work.

Peter began to cry.

Wendy woke up.

She was very surprised to find a strange boy in her room!

"Why are you crying?" asked Wendy.

"My shadow has come off," said Peter.

"I cannot make it stick on again."

Wendy got out of bed.

She went to her sewing box.

She found a needle and some thread.

Wendy sewed Peter's shadow onto his feet.

Peter did not cry again, even though it hurt.

Peter thanked her.

And they introduced each other.

Suddenly, Peter remembered Tinker Bell.

He jumped up and let her out of the drawer.

She was very angry.

"A real fairy!" gasped Wendy.

"I have always wanted to see a fairy."

"Fairies began when the first baby laughed," said Peter.

"Its laugh broke into a thousand pieces.

Each piece became a fairy."

Tinker Bell wanted to leave.

"We must go back to Neverland," she said.

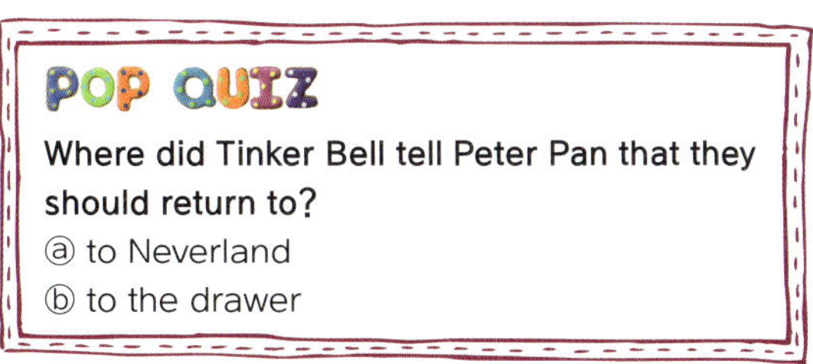

KEY WORDS

- come off
- get out of bed
- sewing box
- needle
- thread
- sew
- even though
- hurt (hurt-hurt-hurt)

- thank
- introduce
- each other
- remember
- jump up
- out of
- real
- gasp

- break into pieces (break-broke-broken)
- thousand
- become (become-became-become)
- leave (leave-left-left)
- go back (go-went-gone)

"Neverland?" asked Wendy.

"What's that?"

"It's where we live," said Peter.

"There are lots of boys there.

They are called the Lost Boys, and they need a

mother. **Aha!**

Go with us, Wendy!

You can look after the Lost Boys.

I will teach you to fly."

Wendy wanted to learn how to fly.

"Can John and Michael, my brothers, go, too?"

she asked.

Peter nodded.

Wendy went to John's bed.

"Wake up!" she said.

"It is time to have an adventure."

She went to Michael's bed.

He was the baby of the family.

"Wake up," she said.

"There is a fairy here to see you."

John and Michael sat up and rubbed their eyes.

KEY WORDS

- lots of
- lost
- **teach** (teach-taught-taught)
- learn
- nod
- have an adventure
- baby
- rub

"Who is he?" said John.

He pointed at Peter Pan.

"This is Peter. 

He will teach us how to fly," said Wendy.

"Fly! Fly!" said Michael.

He bounced up and down on his bed.

Then, Michael fell off and landed on the floor with a bump.

"I can't fly," he said sadly.

"You need some fairy dust," said Peter.

He took a small bag from his belt.

There was golden dust in it.

He shook the dust over Michael.

"Now, move your shoulders," he said.

"Think about flying."

Michael moved his shoulders.

"I will think about flying to the moon," he said.

He flapped his arms.

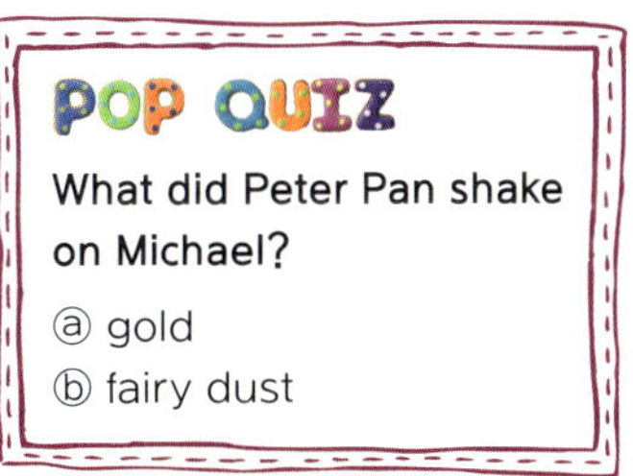

KEY WORDS

- bounce up and down
- fall (fall-fell-fallen)
- floor
- with a bump
- dust

- golden
- shake (shake-shook-shaken)
- move
- shoulder
- flap one's arms

A moment later, Michael floated off the bed!

He began to fly around the room.

Peter shook some fairy dust onto John and Wendy.

They began to fly, too.

John went up to the ceiling and bumped his head.

"Go with me to Neverland," said Peter.

He led the children to the open window.

One by one, they flew into the sky.

Nana was far below them.

She barked and barked, but the children were gone.

- **lead** (lead-led-led)
- one by one
- far below
- gone

Chapter Two

Comprehension Quiz

A Which of the following does Peter Pan have? Choose all that apply.

shadow

sewing box

fairy dust

Nana

B Mark T for true or F for false.

❶ Wendy was angry to find Peter in her room.   T F

❷ The Lost Boys lived in London.   T F

❸ Peter wanted Wendy to look after the Lost Boys.   T F

❹ Nana flew into the sky.   T F

C Choose the best answer to each question.

❶ Why did Peter Pan visit Wendy's room again?

    a) to find some soap

    b) to find his shadow

    c) to find a fairy

    d) to find some bells

❷ Who put Peter Pan's shadow in the drawer?

    a) Wendy   b) Michael

    c) Nana   d) Tinker Bell

D Fill in each blank with the right word below.

shoulders	feet	eyes	head

❶ Michael moved his __________ and thought about flying.

❷ John bumped his __________ on the ceiling.

❸ Wendy sewed Peter's shadow back onto his __________.

❹ John and Michael rubbed their __________.

Neverland

"How do we get to Neverland?" called Wendy.

"Fly toward that star."

Peter pointed at a star in the distance.

"Then, we go straight ahead until morning." said Peter.

After a while, Wendy noticed that they were flying over the sea.

She saw an island below them.

"I can see mermaids!" she said.

"I can see some wolves," said John.

He sounded frightened.

KEY WORDS

- get to
- toward
- in the distance
- straight
- ahead
- until
- notice
- island
- mermaid
- frightened
- loud
- boom
- Watch out!
- huge
- cannonball
- pirate ship
- almost
- hit (hit-hit-hit)

"What is that boat?" asked Michael.

He pointed at a big ship.

A moment later, there was a loud boom.

"Watch out!" shouted Peter.

A huge cannonball flew up into the air.

It came from the pirate ship below.

It almost hit the children.

Down below on the ship, the pirate captain
stroked his beard.

"Is that Peter Pan?" he said to himself.

"I have been waiting a long time to fight him." Aha!

He looked at his right arm.

Instead of a hand, there was a large hook.

His name was Captain Hook.

He was a very cruel man.

He had lost his hand in a battle with Peter Pan.

Peter had fed it to a crocodile.

Now, the crocodile followed Captain Hook around.

It wanted to eat the rest of him.

So Captain Hook hated Peter.

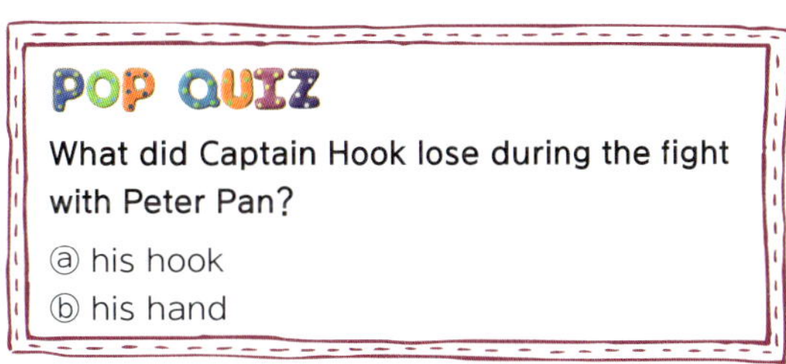

KEY WORDS

- down below
- captain
- stroke one's beard
- **say to oneself** (say-said-said)
- wait
- **fight** (fight-fought-fought)
- instead of
- hook

- cruel
- **lose** (lose-lost-lost)
- battle
- **feed** (feed-fed-fed)
- crocodile
- follow around
- rest of
- hate

Captain Hook was not the only person watching the sky.

The Lost Boys were in the forest.

They had their bows and arrows ready.

One of them was called Nibs.

He saw something strange flying in the air.

It looked like a big, white bird.

Really, it was Wendy wearing a night dress.

But Nibs did not know that.

- only
- bow
- arrow
- ready
- look like
- really
- night dress
- **shoot** (shoot-shot-shot)
- jealous
- raise

Tinker Bell flew down.

"Peter wants you to shoot that big, white bird,"
she said.

"It is called a Wendy Bird."

Tinker Bell was jealous.

She thought that Peter liked Wendy more than
her.

Nibs raised his bow and shot an arrow at Wendy.

Moments later, Wendy fell to the ground.

The Lost Boys crowded around.

They saw an arrow in her chest.

"Is it dead?" asked one of them.

"That is not a bird," said another.

"It looks like a girl.

We should not have listened to Tinker Bell."

Suddenly, they heard Peter's voice.

"Hello, boys!" said Peter as he landed.

"I have brought you a mother."

"I think I have killed her," said Nibs.

Peter knelt by Wendy.

"She is still alive," he said.

"But why did you shoot her?"

"Tinker Bell told me to do it," said Nibs.

Peter was angry with Tinker Bell.

"Go away!" he said.

"I never want to see you again."

- crowd around
- chest
- dead (↔ alive)
- another
- should have + p.p.
- bring (bring-brought-brought)
- kill
- kneel (kneel-knelt-knelt)
- Go away!
- never

John and Michael dropped down out of the sky.

"What happened?" they asked.

Peter explained.

"We will build her a house."

The Lost Boys quickly built a house around
Wendy.

They built it from branches and moss.

Wendy lived in the house and got better.

She liked to visit the Lost Boys in their house.

They lived underground, beneath a big, old tree.

Wendy told them stories and looked after them.

They all loved her—all except Tinker Bell.

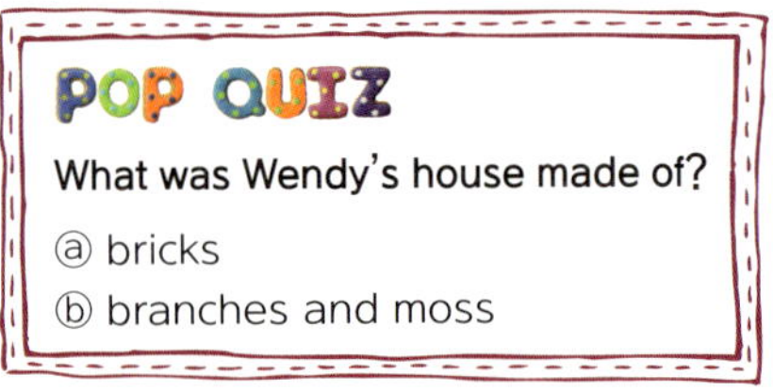

KEY WORDS

- drop down out of
- What happened?
- explain
- **build** (build-built-built)
- quickly

- branch
- moss
- get better
- underground
- beneath

- except
- one day
- get dark
- oar
- splash

One day, Wendy and the boys went to a rock by
the sea.

They lay in the sun and fell asleep.

It began to get dark.

Wendy heard a strange sound.

It sounded like the oars of a boat.

They were splashing in the water.

"Peter, wake up!" said Wendy.

"Pirates!"

Peter jumped up.

"We must hide."

Everyone hid.

They watched the boat as it came nearer.

Two pirates were in it, along with a girl called
Tiger Lily.

They had tied her up.

They wanted to leave her on the rock.

KEY WORDS

- **hide** (hide-hid-hidden)
- **nearer**
- **along with**
- **tie up**
- **leave ... alone**
- **set free** (set-set-set)
- **speak** (speak-spoke-spoken)
- **let ... go**

Just then, Peter began to shout.

His voice sounded like Captain Hook's!

"Leave her alone," he called.

"Set Tiger Lily free."

The pirates thought that Captain Hook was
speaking.

They let Tiger Lily go.

A few minutes later, the real Captain Hook came along.

"Why did you let Tiger Lily go?" he yelled.

"I told you to tie her up and to leave her on the rock.

The sea will come and drown her."

"But you told us to let her go," said one of the pirates.

"No, I did not!" roared Captain Hook.

Peter watched the men arguing.

He should have kept quiet.

But he was proud of what he had done. **Aha!**

He shouted, "It was me! I told them to let her go."

KEY WORDS

- come along
- yell
- drown
- roar
- argue

- keep quiet
- rush over
- attack
- wound
- realize

- terrified
- rush away
- lucky
- escape

Captain Hook rushed over to the rock.

He attacked Peter with his hook and wounded him.

He was about to kill Peter when he realized that the crocodile was coming.

Captain Hook was terrified and rushed away.

Peter had a lucky escape.

Comprehension Quiz

Chapter Three

A Circle the right word(s) for each underlined part.

❶ A (<u>crocodile / tiger</u>) wanted to eat Captain Hook.

❷ Peter Pan was (<u>angry / pleased</u>) with Tinker Bell.

❸ Captin Hook attacked Peter Pan with his (<u>hand / hook</u>).

❹ The pirates wanted to leave (<u>Tiger Lily / Tinker Bell</u>) on the rock.

B Mark T for true or F for false.

❶ Nibs shot Wendy because Tinker Bell told him to do that.   T F

❷ The Lost Boys built the house around Peter Pan.   T F

❸ Tinker Bell loved Wendy.   T F

❹ Captain Hook told the pirates to let Tiger Lily go.   T F

 Choose the best answer to each question.

❶ What is NOT right about Captain Hook?

a) He had a beard.

b) He had a hook instead of his hand.

c) He was a very friendly man.

d) He hated Peter Pan.

❷ Why did Tinker Bell lie to Nibs?

a) She did not know that it was Wendy.

b) She was jealous of Wendy.

c) She knew that Peter wanted to hurt Wendy.

d) She thought that the bird had stolen Wendy's night dress.

❸ Why could NOT Captain Hook kill Peter Pan?

a) He felt sorry for Peter Pan.

b) The pirates told him to let Peter Pan go.

c) Peter Pan wounded him with a sword.

d) The crocodile scared him away.

Prisoners on the Pirate Ship

Neverland was an exciting place to live. Aha!

But Wendy, John, and Michael missed their parents.

"I want to go home," said Wendy one evening.

Everyone was gathered underground.

The only way in and out was to climb through hollow tree trunks.

"We want to go with you," begged the Lost Boys.

KEY WORDS

- prisoner
- exciting
- gather
- in and out
- climb
- hollow
- tree trunk
- beg
- suppose
- frown at

They loved Wendy and her stories.

They loved having a mother to look after them.

Wendy smiled.

"I suppose you can."

"Well, I am not going."

Peter frowned at them all.

"You can all go, but I will stay here.

Tinker Bell will show you how to get home."

Wendy and the boys climbed up the hollow tree trunks.

But Captain Hook and his pirates were waiting for them.

They caught each boy as he came out of the tree.

They caught Wendy, too.

All of the children were tied up.

The pirates shut them into Wendy's little house.

Then, they picked up the entire house.

They carried it to the pirate ship.

But Captain Hook stayed behind.

He climbed down the hollow tree trunk into the underground home.

Peter was fast asleep on the bed in his room.

A cup was on the table next to him.

Captain Hook had some poison.

He wanted to put it into Peter's mouth.

He tried to reach Peter, but the roots were in the way.

He could only reach the cup.

KEY WORDS

- come out of
- pick up
- entire
- carry
- stay behind
- be fast asleep
- poison
- reach
- root
- be in the way

So Captain Hook put a few drops of poison into
the cup.

Then, he went away.

After a while, Peter woke up.

"I'm thirsty," he said.

"I will have a drink from my cup."

Suddenly, Tinker Bell flew down into the room.

She told Peter that the children were on the pirate
ship.

"I will rescue them!" said Peter.

"But first I will have a drink."

KEY WORDS

- a few drops of
- thirsty
- have a drink
- rescue
- believe
- make trouble
- lift
- to one's lips
- snatch

"No! The cup has poison in it," said Tinker Bell.

"I do not believe you," said Peter.

"You are just trying to make more trouble."

He lifted the cup to his lips.

"No!" said Tinker Bell again.

She snatched the cup from him.

She drank all the poison.

Tinker Bell fell to the ground.

Her light grew fainter.

Peter forgot that he had been angry with Tinker Bell.

"You saved my life," he said.

"I will not let you die."

He knew a way to help her.

All the children in the world must say, "I believe in fairies."

They must clap their hands.

Then, Tinker Bell would be well again.

Peter shouted as loud as he could. Aha!

And somehow all of the children heard him.

All over the world, they shouted, "I believe in fairies."

Tinker Bell's light grew stronger.

She sat up.

She wanted Peter to stay with her.

"No," said Peter.

"Thank you for saving me.

Now, I must go to save the others."

He set off for the pirate ship at once.

KEY WORDS

- fainter
- **forget** (forget-forgot-forgotten)
- save
- life
- die
- believe in
- clap hands

- be well
- somehow
- all over the world
- stronger
- set off
- at once

On the pirate ship, Wendy and the boys were tied up.

"Some of you can be pirates on my ship," said Captain Hook.

"The rest of you must walk the plank."

"What does that mean?" asked Michael.

"It means that you walk out on a plank of wood and jump into the sea," laughed Captain Hook.

"But I can't swim!" said Michael.

"Don't worry," whispered Wendy.

"Peter will save us."

"Peter Pan is dead!" said Captain Hook.

"He will not save you."

A pirate tied Wendy to the mast.

"You will be the last to go," said the captain.

"You can watch them die."

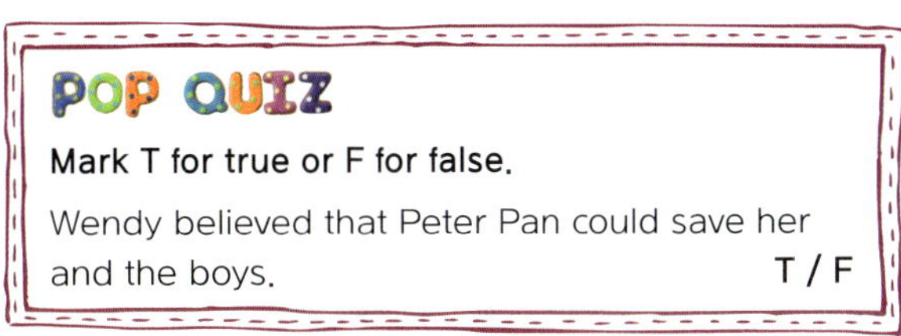

Captain Hook did not know that Peter was

climbing up the side of the ship!

Peter hid in a corner and made a crowing noise.

He sounded like a cockerel.

"Doodle-doo!"

"What is that?" said Captain Hook.

"It's the deadly doodle-doo!" said one of the

pirates.

"I have heard stories about it.

It kills pirates!"

The other pirates turned pale. Aha!

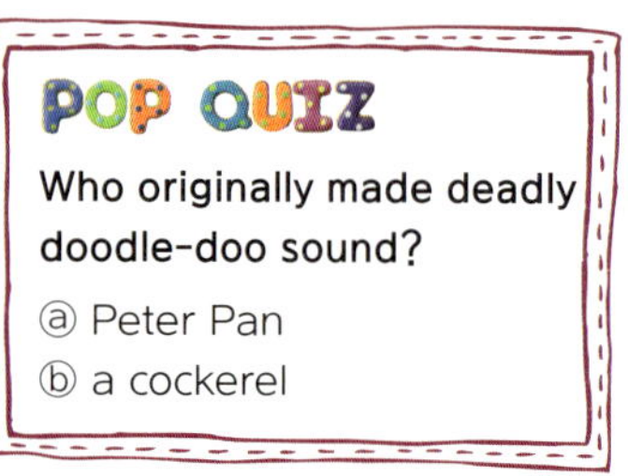

KEY WORDS

- side
- corner
- crow
- noise

- cockerel
- doodle-doo
- deadly
- pale

- search for
- everywhere
- go off
- sword

The pirates began to search everywhere for the deadly doodle-doo.

But they could not find it.

"I will find the deadly doodle-doo," said Captain Hook.

He went off, with his sword ready.

Peter crept out of his hiding place.

The pirates were not looking.

He had a sword.

He cut the ropes that held Wendy to the mast.

"Let me wear your cloak," he whispered.

"I will stand by the mast.

Captain Hook will think I am you.

I will give him a surprise!"

So Wendy crept away and untied the boys.

Peter stood by the mast while wearing her cloak.

Suddenly, he jumped and gave a loud cry.

"Doodle-doo!"

"It's the girl!" shouted the pirates.

"She is the deadly doodle-doo!"

KEY WORDS

- **creep out of** (creep-crept-crept)
- **cut** (cut-cut-cut)
- **cloak**
- **stand by** (stand-stood-stood)
- **surprise**
- **creep away**
- **untie**
- **give a cry** (give-gave-given)

Chapter Four

Comprehension Quiz

A Who said what? Match each line with the right person.

❶ 

• a) "Peter will save us."

❷ 

• b) "I will find the deadly doodle-doo."

❸ 

• c) "Captain Hook will think I am you."

B Fill in each blank with the right word(s) below.

cloak	house	pirate ship	poison

❶ Tinker Bell drank the ___________.

❷ Peter wore Wendy's ___________.

❸ Peter climbed up the side of the ___________.

❹ The pirates carried Wendy's ___________ to the pirate ship.

C Choose the best answer to each question.

❶ Why did the Lost Boys want to go with Wendy?

a) They loved Wendy and her stories.

b) They missed their parents.

c) They did not like living in Neverland.

d) They could not get into their underground home.

❷ Why could NOT Captain Hook put poison in Peter Pan's mouth?

a) Peter's mouth was closed.

b) Captain Hook could not get close enough.

c) Tinker Bell got in the way.

d) Captain Hook did not want to kill Peter.

❸ Why did the pirates think that Wendy was the deadly doodle-doo?

a) They thought Wendy made a noise like a cockerel.

b) They thought Wendy killed some pirates.

c) They thought Wendy caught the deadly doodle-doo.

d) They thought Wendy told them a story about it.

Chapter Five

Home Again

The pirates rushed toward the mast.

Peter threw off the cloak.

He drew his sword.

Captain Hook gasped.

"I thought you were dead!"

"Do I look dead?" asked Peter.

He shouted for the boys to come and help.

KEY WORDS

- throw off
- draw a sword (draw-drew-drawn)
- look for

- weapon
- win (win-won-won)

The pirates looked for their weapons.

The boys had picked them up!

Peter said, "Leave Captain Hook to me!"

Peter and Captain Hook fought each other.

Both of them were good at fighting. Aha!

At first, Peter was winning.

Then, Captain Hook was winning.

At last, Peter hurt the Captain Hook with his sword.

Captain Hook climbed up on the edge of the ship.

"You will never win!" he roared.

But then he lost his balance.

He fell off the ship into the sea.

The hungry crocodile was waiting for him.

The other pirates jumped into the sea as well.

Peter and the boys had won!

"Now we shall live on this ship," said Peter.

"We will be pirates together."

"No," said Wendy.

"I want to go home.

John and Michael will go with me."

"We want to go, too," said the Lost Boys.

Peter was sad.

He did not want them to go back to London.

But Peter Pan and Tinker Bell flew back to
London.

The others followed them.

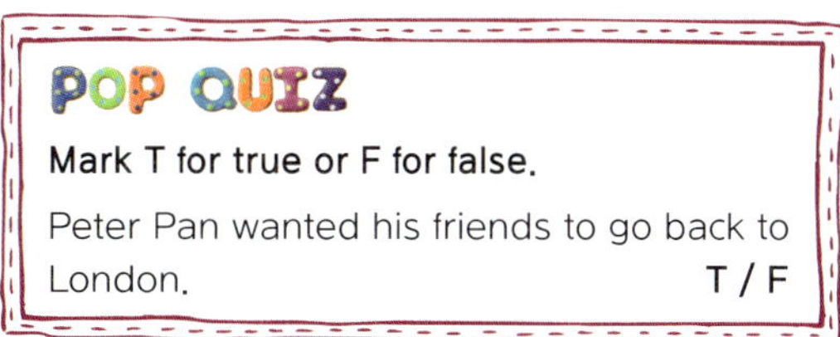

At last, Wendy, John and Michael arrived at the
house.

Mrs. Darling always left the window open in case
her children came home.

Now they flew in through the window.

"Have I been here before?" asked Michael.

He did not remember his home.

"Of course you have," said John.

"Let's get into our beds," said Wendy.

"It will be a surprise for Mother."

A little while later, the door opened.

Mrs. Darling came to the bedroom every night.

She missed her children.

She wished they would come home.

She thought they were gone forever.

When she saw them in their beds, she cried out.

"Is this a dream?" she asked.

"No, Mother," said Wendy.

"We are home again!" They jumped out of bed and hugged their mother.

She hugged them back.

KEY WORDS

- arrive at
- in case
- of course
- get into

- wish
- be gone
- forever
- cry out

- dream
- hug

The noise brought Mr. Darling running. 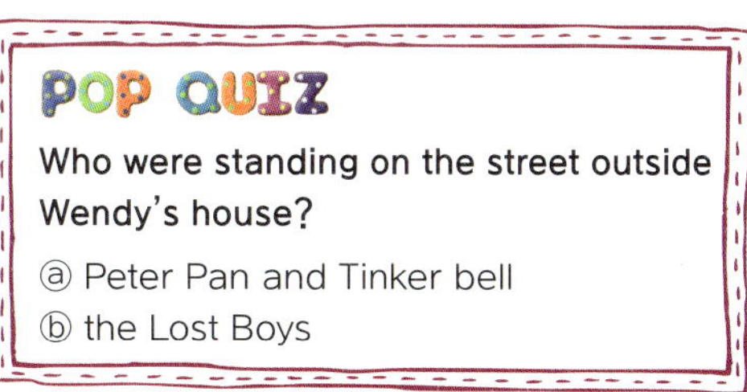

He hugged them, too.

Wendy tugged at his sleeve.

"We have brought some friends with us," she said.

"Look out the window."

Mr. Darling looked out the window.

There on the street stood the Lost Boys.

Mrs. Darling ran downstairs to let them in.

"You can stay with us," she said.

KEY WORDS

- tug at
- sleeve
- look out
- street
- let in

Outside the bedroom window, Peter Pan waited.

"You can stay too," said Wendy.

"But if I stay, I will grow up," said Peter. 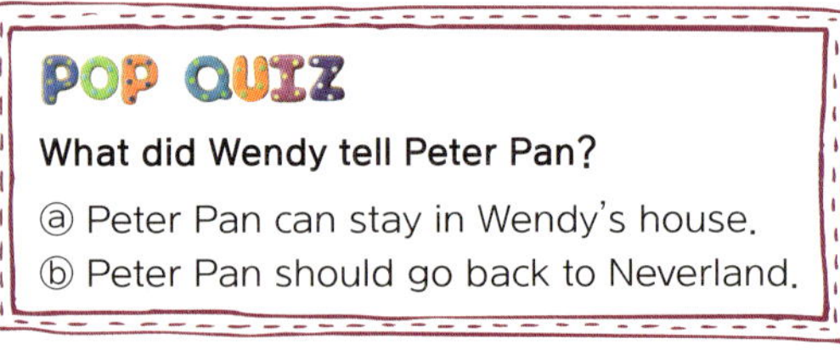

"I never want to grow up."

Tinker Bell flew around his head.

She tugged at his arm.

"I will go back to Neverland," said Peter.

"But I will come back and see you one day."

KEY WORDS

▪ come back

Wendy watched as Peter flew into the sky.

"Goodbye," she whispered.

She would wait for him until he came back.

Peter and Tinker Bell flew toward a star in the distance.

They flew straight ahead until morning.

A Circle the right word(s) for each underlined part.

❶ Peter and Captain Hook were both (<u>good / poor</u>) at fighting.

❷ Mrs. Darling always left the window (<u>open / closed</u>) in the children's bedroom.

❸ The hungry crocodile was waiting for (<u>Peter Pan / Captain Hook</u>).

❹ Wendy, John and Michael were in bed when their (<u>father / mother</u>) came in.

B Mark T for true or F for false.

❶ The Lost Boys wanted to go to London with Wendy. ☐ T ☐ F

❷ Peter really wanted to grow up. ☐ T ☐ F

❸ John remembered his home. ☐ T ☐ F

❹ Mrs. Darling came to the children's bedroom once a week. ☐ T ☐ F

 Choose the best answer to each question.

❶ Why did Captain Hook think Peter Pan was dead?

    a) He thought that the deadly doodle-doo had caught Peter.

    b) He saw Peter asleep and thought that he was dead.

    c) He thought that his pirates had killed Peter.

    d) He thought that Peter had drunk the poison.

❷ Why did Peter Pan say, "Leave Captain Hook to me!"?

    a) He wanted to fight Captain Hook himself.

    b) He did not want Captain Hook to get hurt.

    c) He wanted to help Captain Hook to escape.

    d) He wanted to show Captain Hook the deadly doodle-doo.

D Put the sentences in order.

❶ Wendy said that Peter Pan could stay in her house.

❷ Wendy, John and Michael flew in through the window from Neverland.

❸ Peter Pan and Tinker Bell went back to Neverland.

❹ Wendy, John and Michael hugged their mother.

_________ → _______ → _______ → _______

Let's Review the Story

Fill in the blanks to review the story.

Title: Peter Pan

Main Characters:

Peter Pan, W______, John, Michael, Captain ______, Tinker Bell, the Lost Boys

Sequence:

1. ______ takes Wendy, John, and Michael to ______.

2. Tinker Bell tells Nibs to s______ Wendy.

3. Wendy looks after the ______ in Neverland.

4. Captain ______ and his pirates catch Wendy, John, Michael, and the Lost Boys.

5. ______ rescues the children, and a c______ waits for Captain Hook to catch him.

6. Wendy, John, Michael, and the Lost Boys go back to London.

7. Peter Pan and Tinker bell go back to ______ because Peter Pan doesn't want to ______.

Let's Think & Talk

Think about the following questions and answer them freely.

❶ If you had fairy dust that made you fly like Peter Pan, where would you want to fly to?

❷ If you were Peter Pan, how would you save Wendy and the children from the pirate ship?

❸ If you could go to Neverland, whom would you want to go with? Tell us the reason.

❹ Do you want to grow up quickly? Or do you want to stay as you are now? Explain the reason.

Let's Review the Story

Title: Peter Pan

Main Characters:

Peter Pan, Wendy , John, Michael, Captain Hook ,

Tinker Bell, the Lost Boys

Sequence:

1. Peter Pan takes Wendy, John, and Michael to Neverland .
2. Tinker Bell tells Nibs to shoot Wendy.
3. Wendy looks after the Lost Boys in Neverland.
4. Captain Hook and his pirates catch Wendy, John, Michael, and the Lost Boys.
5. Peter Pan rescues the children, and a crocodile waits for Captain Hook to catch him.
6. Wendy, John, Michael, and the Lost Boys go back to London.
7. Peter Pan and Tinker bell go back to Neverland because Peter Pan doesn't want to grow up .

After-reading Test

- Peter Pan
- Level 2
- 19 Questions

  (Vocabulary 5 / Reading Comprehension 10 /

  Sentence Structure & Grammar 4)

1. What does "plank" mean?

    The rest of you must walk the plank.

    ① a thick rope
    ② a street
    ③ a heavy gun
    ④ a long flat piece of wood

2. Which is NOT a pair of words that are opposites?
    ① roar ↔ whisper
    ② set off ↔ arrive at
    ③ catch ↔ carry
    ④ dead ↔ alive

3. Which pair has the wrong past tense form of the listed verb?
    ① teach − taught   ② hit − hitted
    ③ set − set   ④ fight − fought

4. Which of the following sentence indicates the feeling that the pirates feel?

    The other pirates turned pale.

    ① frightened   ② jealous
    ③ proud   ④ exciting

5. Choose the right word for the blank.

    Why do we have a dog to take care _______ our children?

    ① like   ② after
    ③ of   ④ with

6. Which house do the Darlings live in?
   ① They lived in a tall, wide house.
   ② They lived in a short, narrow house.
   ③ They lived in a tall, narrow house.
   ④ They lived in a short, wide house.

7. Choose all the reasons that Wendy wants to keep on sharing the bedroom with her little brothers.
   ① They had fun together.
   ② She had a big bed.
   ③ She felt safe because Nana stayed with them.
   ④ She liked the stories her brothers told.

8. What happened to Mr. Darling's trousers after he got ready to go out?
   ① The trousers were too big.
   ② The trousers were covered with dog hairs.
   ③ The trousers were not long enough.
   ④ The trousers were full of holes.

9. The night when Mr. and Mrs. Darling went out, what did Wendy lying on the bed hear?
   ① her parents talking
   ② Peter Pan crying
   ③ John and Michael snoring
   ④ Nana barking

10. What did Peter Pan shake on Wendy and the children to let them fly?
   ① golden dust
   ② snow
   ③ water
   ④ poison

11. What animal tried to eat Captain Hook?

① dog

② tiger

③ wolf

④ crocodile

12. Which place in Neverland did the Lost Boys live in?

① They lived on a rock by the sea.

② They lived in Wendy' s house.

③ They lived in on a pirate ship.

④ They lived underground beneath a big, old tree.

13. Why did Wendy, John and Michael want to go back home from Neverland?

① They missed their parents.

② Neverland was not an exciting place to live.

③ They did not like Peter Pan.

④ They were afraid of the pirates.

14. Why did Tinker Bell drink poison in the cup instead of Peter Pan?

① She wanted to make sure that Peter should not drink it.

② She did not know it was poison.

③ She knew that poison would not harm a fairy.

④ She wanted to make herself ill.

15. Where did Peter Pan and Tinker Bell return at the end?

① They went to the moon.

② They went to Neverland.

③ They went to another house in London.

④ They went to a different city.

※ Choose the wrong part of the sentence. (16∼17)

16.
> <u>Both</u> of <u>them</u> <u>were good at</u> <u>to fight</u>.
>   ①   ②   ③   ④

17.
> <u>He</u> <u>should have</u> <u>keep</u> <u>quiet</u>.
> ①   ②   ③ ④

※ Choose the correct word or phrase for each blank. (18∼19)

18.
> If I ____________, I will grow up.

① will stay   ② stay
③ stayed   ④ staying

19.
> Time ________ your medicine.

① taking   ② took
③ to take   ④ taken

Sarah J. Dodd
Sarah J. Dodd is an experienced primary school teacher who resides in the UK, but has also taught in Australia. She has a PhD in Science and a certificate in Creative Writing. She has published four books for younger children — 'An Angel Anyway' (Anyway Press) and the Little Angels' series (Lion Hudson plc). Her children's Bible will be published in 2015. She is currently working on a novel for 9-12 year olds and another for young adults.

Peter Pan

Written by James Matthew Barrie
Retold by Sarah J. Dodd
Illustrated by Yu Kang Kim

First published May 2015
2nd publishing August 2022

Publisher: Kyudo Chung
Editors: Juyon Choi, Jiyeong Park, Kyunghee Jang
Designer: Eunhee Lee

Published and distributed by
Happy House, an Imprint of DARAKWON, Inc.
Darakwon Bldg., 211 Munbal-ro, Paju-si, Gyeonggi-do, 10881, Republic of Korea
Tel: 82-2-736-2031(ext. 250)   Fax: 82-2-732-2037
Homepage: www.ihappyhouse.co.kr

ISBN: 978-89-6653-191-2 18740 / 978-89-6653-156-1 18740(set)

[Components]
• 1 Audio CD (Recording Studio: Aram)
• Answer Keys & Korean Translation: Free download at www.ihappyhouse.co.kr